NICK BUTTERWORTH AND MICK INKPEN

STORIES JESUS TOLD

D

To help people understand what God is like, Jesus told lots of stories which are as exciting today as when they were first heard.

The Ten Silver Coins is still a great favourite and its message is one that children especially love to hear.

Marshall Pickering
An Imprint of HarperCollins*Publishers*
77-85 Fulham Palace Road,
Hammersmith, London W6 8JB
1 3 5 7 9 10 8 6 4 2

First published in Great Britain
in 1989 by Marshall Pickering

This edition published in 1995

A catalogue record for this book is
available from the British Library

0 551 02882-3

Printed and bound in **Hong Kong**

Co-edition arranged by Angus Hudson Ltd, London

The Ten Silver Coins

Nick Butterworth and Mick Inkpen

HarperCollins*Publishers*

Here is a woman. She has ten silver coins. She likes to count them.

One, two, three, four...

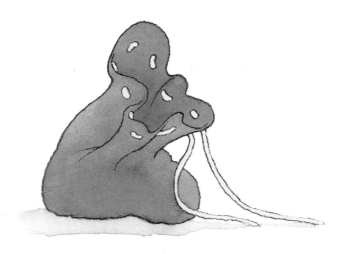

Oops! Silly cat! Now they've
gone all over the place.

The woman picks up her silver coins. They have been scattered everywhere!

The cat doesn't care. He has stretched out and gone to sleep.

The woman counts her silver coins again. But there are only nine. Bother! One of them is missing.

Never mind, it can't have gone far.

Perhaps it is under the rug.
No. There is no sign of it there.

Perhaps it has bounced into the fireplace. Carefully she sifts through the ashes.

What a messy job! But no, there is no coin.

Perhaps it rolled right under the door and out into the garden.

She searches and searches, but she cannot find the coin anywhere.

She even looks inside her pots and pans, even though she really knows it can't be there.

Clatter! Bang! What a noise she is making!

She's making so much noise, she's woken up the cat. Serves him right. He's off to find a quiet spot in the garden.

There it is! The cat was lying on it all the time! The missing silver coin is found!

The woman laughs. She is so happy she calls a friend to tell her the good news.

Jesus says, 'We are like the woman's silver coins. God wants every single one of us.'

HAMILTON
COLLEGE

You can read the story of
The Ten Silver Coins in Luke
chapter 15 verses 8 to 10.